I0210651

New Day
Christian Education, Inc.

Life After Divorce

The Pathway to Wholeness

By Merlin & Shawner English

New Day
Christian Education, Inc.

Life After Divorce: The Pathway to Wholeness

Copyright © 2012 by Merlin & Shawner English. All rights reserved

Scripture quotations marked KJV are taken from the *The Holy Bible,* King James Version.

Scripture quotations marked NIV are taken from the Holy Bible, *New International Version,*®NIV.® Copyright © 1984 by Biblica, Inc.™

Disclaimer

New Day Christian Education, Inc. is not a Marriage and Family Counseling service. The Christian educational training programs and services provided by New Day Christian Education, Inc. are not designed or intended to take the place of certified marriage and family counseling. Our curriculum is intended for the purpose of Christian education, Christian development, and personal enrichment. Results from our educational products and services are based on individual effort and other factors.

CONTENTS

Notes

_____

_____

_____

_____

_____

_____

_____

_____

_____

_____

_____

_____

_____

_____

_____

_____

_____

_____

_____

_____

_____

_____

Introduction

"It Happened to Me" & "It Happened to Me Too"

This manual is an educational document that will provide the necessary tools for a person who is separated or divorced to begin picking up the pieces of their life and move to a place of wholeness (true singleness). It will help them move forward and fulfill their purpose in life.

Our founding scripture is Luke 4:18-19 (companion text Isa 61:1-2) *"The Spirit of the Lord is upon me, because he hath anointed me to preach the gospel to the poor; he hath sent me to heal the brokenhearted, to preach deliverance to the captives, and recovering of sight to the blind, to set at liberty them that are bruised, [19]To preach the acceptable year of the Lord(KJV)."*

In the state of divorce, you are "single-again" so you must learn how to be "single" (whole). If you are separated, although you are not divorced, for the most part you are also single-again and must learn how to be "single" (whole). Therefore, our goal is to give you the tools to become "single" or whole (maybe for the first time ever). **You will have what you need to become "single"—unhurt, restored, intact, free of deformity, and mentally and emotionally sound so that you can become a separate, unique, and whole individual—unbroken and undivided.**

Throughout the course, you will see "single-again" and divorced used interchangeably. The word divorced has such a negative connotation, and can sometimes challenge one's perception of self and self worth. Although being single-again is not what you had envisioned, it is where you are right now. You are not "single" as in never have been married, but you are "single-again" as in no longer married.

Notes

_____

_____

_____

_____

_____

_____

_____

_____

_____

_____

_____

_____

_____

_____

_____

_____

_____

_____

_____

_____

_____

_____

_____

_____

_____

_____

As we delve in the material, take an honest look at yourself. Make up your mind to be free from the effects of your past and present situation. Be committed to move forward in your life and achieve all that God has purposed for your life. Do not just sit back and let life happen to you, take control and make a difference for you and those who depend on you.

We recommend that you take your time and focus on one lesson per week. The time you spend in reflection and answering the questions will build a strong foundation to becoming a single/whole person. For your convenience, we have provided an appendix that includes all of the scriptures we reference. Read the lessons and read the scriptures that accompany each lesson. When you build yourself in the word of God, you build up treasures that last a lifetime.

Roller Coaster Activity

While you were growing up, you may recall all the hype about riding roller coasters. The more dangerous they were the better. You would judge them by how much they jerk you around, turn you upside down, how steep the downward slopes were and how fast they went. You may even remember going to the carnival or theme park to ride your favorites. You may not have liked them at all. But whether you like them or not, you can probably share in vivid detail some of your experiences on them. Unfortunately, your marriage, separation and divorce have taken you on a volatile roller coaster ride. In terms of your experience so far, describe your roller coaster ride of marriage, separation and divorce using the notes page.

Workshop Activity: When you hear a ride that sounds very similar to yours, raise your hand, stand beside your seat, or motion as if you are on the ride.

Notes

Statistics/Rationale

The divorce rate still hovers around 50% (for first marriages), surprisingly, among those who call themselves Christians and non-Christians, alike. The rate increases with each successive marriage. People marry or desire to be married for all sorts of reasons. No matter how noble or not-so-noble the reason, these factors can make or break a relationship. Some reasons people marry, include but are not limited to:

- To be fulfilled or loved
- To satisfy sexual desires
- Getting older—the proverbial clock is ticking
- Have been dating the same person for a while, so it seems like the next logical step
- Somebody prophesied your mate
- To be taken care of financially—security
- To have children
- Already have children together
- Pressure from family and society to get married

There are 3 major causes of divorce:

- **Finance**

  This area is touted as the number one cause of divorce. The conflict may include one spends too much or one is too thrifty, a lot of money or not enough money, different priorities of how money is earned or used, and more.

Notes

_____

_____

_____

_____

_____

_____

_____

_____

_____

_____

_____

_____

_____

_____

_____

_____

_____

_____

_____

_____

_____

_____

_____

_____

_____

- **Communication**

  This may include miscommunication or lack of communication with each other, with regard to rearing children, with regard to family, with regard to in-laws, with regard to friends, etc.

- **Sex**

  This is a very sensitive area. People have a difficult time expressing their needs and desires with regard to sex and intimacy. Unfortunately when not dealt with appropriately, many outcomes result. Some include infidelity, lack of sex, lack of romance, lack of intimacy, a myriad of excuses, and more.

Arguments over which is more potent is not as important as knowing that all three are dangerous and destructive. When honestly considering the demise of your relationship, you will find that it falls in one or more of the categories mentioned above.

Notes

_____

_____

_____

_____

_____

_____

_____

_____

_____

_____

_____

_____

_____

_____

_____

_____

_____

_____

_____

_____

_____

_____

_____

_____

Activity

Take a personal inventory. Be honest with yourself. Acknowledgement, acceptance, and honesty are the beginning steps of healing and wholeness. Using the notes page, answer the following questions:

1. Why did you marry?
2. Did you receive premarital counseling? If so, how long and in-depth was the program?
3. Although there may have been a variety of factors, what was the overall cause(s) of your separation/divorce?
4. Name three positive things you have learned about yourself so far through your process.
5. Name three negative things you have learned about yourself so far through your process.
6. If you could do it all over again, what would you do differently?

Notes

Divorce

According to Wikipedia, divorce is the dissolution of the marriage. It is the final termination or end to a marriage union. It cancels the legal duties and responsibilities of marriage and dissolves the bonds of matrimony between the parties. Divorce is handled differently around the world. As of now, there are still two countries that do not have a civil procedure for divorce: the Philippines and Vatican City. Even within the United States, divorce is handled differently from state to state. Divorce can be very complicated, lengthy, costly, and simply exhausting. It can involve spousal support, child support, child custody, distribution of assets, and division of debts.

To get a better understanding of divorce, let's go back to the beginning. Let's see what the Bible has to say on the matter. Read and study Ex. 21:7-11, Deut. 21: 10-14, Deut. 24:1-4, Ezra 10:1-16, Neh. 13:23-29, Esther 1:10-22, Isa. 50:1, Isa. 54:4, Jer. 3:8, Mat. 5:27-32, Mat. 19:1-12, and 1 Cor. 7:10-17 (Use your Bible, as these passages are not in Appendix A unless used in other sections of the book.) We have highlighted a few below:

Deuteronomy 24:1 states, **"When a man hath taken a wife, and married her, and it come to pass that she find no favour in his eyes, because he hath found some uncleanness in her: then let him write her a bill of divorcement, and give it in her hand, and send her out of his house."**

In order to get a divorce, Moses said that men would have to give wives a bill of divorcement and send her away. Send her away meant that he had to give her money or goods to start life over again. Over the course of time, this was not upheld and women were being sent out with nothing.

In Matthew 19, Jesus came to fulfill the law, or provide the essence and spirit of the law. He referred to Moses' provision of divorce which was given to protect

Notes

women, and he added more. Husbands were leaving wives for any reason (i.e. Nagging, can't cook, just want someone else, anything they didn't like), leaving them destitute with no means to start over in life and no hope for marrying again. Jesus made it clear that under the New Covenant the intentions of your heart are just as important as what you do.

Make no mistake about it, God hates divorce (Mal. 2:14-16)! Divorce is an allowance due to sinful man (Mat. 19:8). It is God's provision, NOT His original intent. God intended and intends for marriage to be permanent. Divorce only happens when one or both parties to the marriage are not truly single (whole).

The Bible shares two reasons for divorce: adultery and abandonment (Mat. 5:31-32; Mat. 19:3-11; 1 Cor. 7:10-17). Even so, divorce is still not a mandate, but an option. Just like anything, you must understand the heart of God. If someone is beating your head in, you need to leave. They could kill you. As a matter of fact, he or she has already abandoned you. According to Bishop Rosie S. O'neal, he or she wants to leave but does not know how, so you need to help them by getting out.

Remember divorce is not the unpardonable sin. 1 John 1:9 says, **"If we confess our sins, he is faithful and just to forgive us our sins, and to cleanse us from all unrighteousness."** Although God hates divorce, He loves the people involved. Don't be in bondage. Even if your divorce does not fit the Biblical reasons for divorce, our God forgives. We serve a loving God, a merciful God, a faithful God, and a forgiving God. God loves you unconditionally. He knows you completely and loves you anyway (Bishop Rosie S. O'neal)!

Notes

Activity

We have discussed the demise of your relationship. Now let's take a closer look at the inner workings or details of the matter. Whether you were the "innocent party" or not you must take full responsibility for the role YOU played in the deterioration of the marriage. It will play a vital part in your quest to be single (whole). Using the notes page answer the following questions:

1. If your spouse was married to a perfect person (let's say Jesus for example), would he (or she) have behaved in such a manner? Of course this is a rhetorical question. The answer is <u>NO</u> (Assuming your spouse was of sound mind)!

2. Every area of your life that is not like Jesus contributed to the failure of your relationship. Now make a list of those areas of your life that is not like Jesus (i.e. Selfishness, argumentative, harsh speech, anger, bitterness, etc.).

3. After making this list, pray to God to deliver you from these things. Work with Him to be all that He created you to be. Keep a journal and make yourself accountable to a trusted friend/mentor to monitor your progress.

Notes

Crisis Time Line (The Slippery Slope)

(The following paragraph and chart are taken from The Fresh Start Divorce Recovery Workbook—Chapter1 by Tom Whiteman & Bob Burns.)

A divorce is much like a death and there is a grieving process. Don't downplay the extent of this grief, as it will only prolong your process. As a matter of fact, it can even shatter your entire belief system. There is nothing wrong with reexamining your beliefs, as it can be a good time of growth for you as you accept some of the complexities of real life and allow God to renew you from the inside out. The recovery process typically goes down before it goes up. And, sometimes you may even have setbacks along the way. The process generally takes about 2 years—some less, some more. Just remember divorce recovery is a process. As a result, there are particular stages that we all go through during this process—denial, anger, bargaining, depression and acceptance. As followers of Christ, along with acceptance, we must forgive! Let's take a closer look at each stage. Elisabeth Kubler-Ross first popularized the stages of grief in her landmark book *On Death and Dying*. She identified five emotional levels that people pass through as they deal with the death of a loved one: denial, anger, bargaining, depression, and acceptance. This theory not only applies to bereavement but also to other tragedies, like divorce.

Notes

_____
_____
_____
_____
_____
_____
_____
_____
_____
_____
_____
_____
_____
_____
_____
_____
_____
_____
_____
_____
_____
_____
_____
_____
_____
_____
_____
_____
_____

CRISIS TIME LINE
(THE SLIPPERY SLOPE)

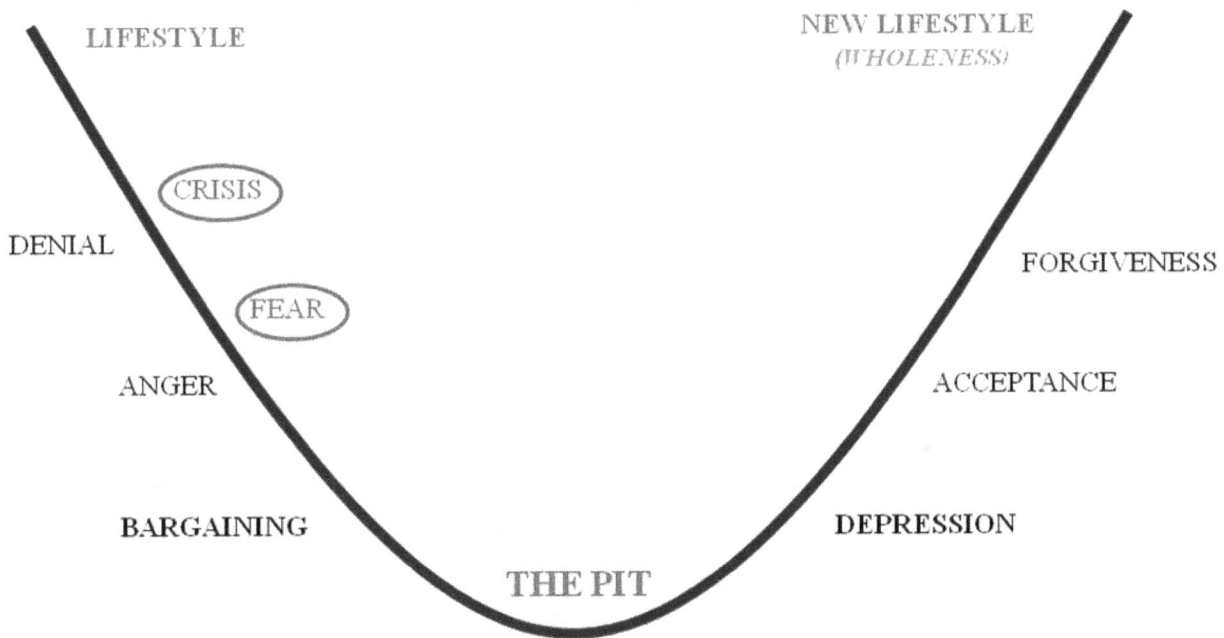

1. Denial: Why is this happening to me? Okay God, how are you going to fix this? Although this is a mess, we won't ever get divorced? It's going to be alright.

    a. "It's not a lack of faith to accept reality. God can work a miracle, but it's foolish to plan your life on the slim chance that he will. The greatest show of faith is to deal with your new reality in the confidence that God will give you strength to do so." (The Fresh Start Divorce Recovery Workbook, p.19)

New Day
Christian Education, Inc.

<u>Notes</u>

_____

_____

_____

_____

_____

_____

_____

_____

_____

_____

_____

_____

_____

_____

_____

_____

_____

_____

_____

_____

_____

_____

_____

_____

_____

_____

_____

2. Anger: Mad/enraged at spouse, fellow Christians, family & friends, yourself and God! Feeling rejection...new friends...new job...relocation...new church home...etc.

    a. Anger, in itself, is not wrong. It matters only how we deal with the feelings of anger. We can deal with anger in the following ways:

        i. Rage: tearing up stuff, hitting a wall or door with your fist, going off on the first person that rubs you the wrong way...wrong answer

        ii. Repression: hold anger inside. This can be more harmful to you—physically harmful even. You need to vent your frustration.

        iii. Redirection: take all your energy and invest it in something positive. Take up a new hobby, attend school, finish a project, etc.

        iv. Resolution: resolve the situations that have made you angry. This may take some time, but at some point, it may be a good idea to discuss your feelings with your ex just to clear the air and get rid of bad feelings toward your ex. If this is not possible, then take it to God and leave it there...just get free!

New Day
Christian Education, Inc.

Notes

3. Bargaining: trying to find a simple solution to a complex problem. How can I make this pain go away? Just come back home and I promise I will never ask questions. God, if you just help me through this.

   a. "True reconciliation requires changes in attitudes and behavior. It is not merely a matter of moving back in together. Go beyond his or her words; watch for changes in behavior, along with a willingness to work on the issue." (The Fresh Start Divorce Recovery Workbook, p.32)

4. Depression: you hit bottom. You realize your efforts are worthless. You are helpless to change your spouse or your situation.

   a. Many times, hitting bottom is what causes us to look up. This is a stage of the process but you can and will come through it. It is necessary but it needs to be monitored. If it gets out of control or last too long, you must seek counsel immediately. Don't be ashamed or afraid to seek help. Be honest about your feelings. This is where you really begin to face reality, seek God in a special way, open up to friends, attend divorce recovery seminar or counsel.

Notes

_____
_____
_____
_____
_____
_____
_____
_____
_____
_____
_____
_____
_____
_____
_____
_____
_____
_____
_____
_____
_____
_____
_____
_____
_____
_____
_____

5. Acceptance and forgiveness: the ex has no hold on you. The mention of their name or occasional meeting does not set you off. The ex can no longer ruin your day or push your buttons. You don't hate your ex.

   a. The relationship is totally redefined. Your ex's personality or character flaws are not your problem anymore. You will be content (not complacent) in your new reality or situation. "The key to recovery is in making wise decisions now about how you're going to live and what you are going to believe about yourself." (The Fresh Start Divorce Recovery Workbook, p.43)

Notes

_____

_____

_____

_____

_____

_____

_____

_____

_____

_____

_____

_____

_____

_____

_____

_____

_____

_____

_____

_____

_____

_____

Activity

Using the notes page answer the following questions:

1. Share the process of your separation and/or divorce in terms of the stages of recovery (denial, anger, bargaining, depression, acceptance & forgiveness).

2. What stage do you think is most difficult to deal with?

3. Where do you see yourself right now on the slippery slope of these stages?

4. Are there significant persons who have supported you? Who are they? How have they supported you?

Notes

_____
_____
_____
_____
_____
_____
_____
_____
_____
_____
_____
_____
_____
_____
_____
_____
_____
_____
_____
_____
_____
_____
_____
_____
_____
_____

Emotions and Self-image

Being single-again is a difficult process. Most often your self-image is at an all-time low. Your emotions are in free fall. From one moment to the next, your mind is all over the place. You do not know who you are and what you are doing from day to day. Many times, you just exist in the shell of a person that you once were. You feel unlovable, like no one cares, like no one will ever want you, like you have nothing to offer, like you are all used up and there is no hope.

Men and women use various things to cover these feelings. Some alienate themselves from the world. They may do the basics like bathe, work, and grocery shopping but they stay away from social venues, friends and family. Others begin dating and dating a lot, thinking that someone else will fill the void and make them feel better. Some become workaholics, delving deeply into work as this may be an area that they can control and find appreciation and gratification. Still others may turn all their attention to the children, living vicariously through them. Some may even turn to the church, giving all their time and attention to the things of God and the work of the ministry. However, they may not ever get to the root of their feelings as all of these are simply masks or band aids for the blood-gushing wounds of a failed marriage.

The good news is you do not have to stay in this state of mind on the emotional roller coaster. You are more than a conqueror (Rom. 8:37). You are the apple of God's eye (Zech. 2:8, Ps. 17: 8). You are the best part of His creation. You are fearfully and wonderfully made (Ps. 139:14). He is concerned about every part of you—even down to the strands of hair on your head (Luke 12:7). He loves you unconditionally!

Notes

_____
_____
_____
_____
_____
_____
_____
_____
_____
_____
_____
_____
_____
_____
_____
_____
_____
_____
_____
_____
_____
_____
_____
_____

Therefore watch your mouth (Prov. 18:21). Speak what God says about you. Speak life. You must love yourself. A healthy self-image is paramount to achieving singleness (wholeness)—Mat. 22:37-40.

You have to accept who God made you. Be happy with you. Discover YOU, accept YOU and be confident in YOU. God made you and, after doing so, saw all of his creation not as "good" but "very good" (Gen. 1:31). You can respect others' opinions of you but you should NOT be moved or ruled by them. You must stand on your own two feet and be confident in the very good thing that God created…YOU!

Endeavor to grow, develop, and improve yourself. Take an honest assessment of where you are. Invest in bettering yourself (i.e. College or trade school, self-help books, conferences, seminars, workshops, etc.)

Activity

Using the notes page answer the following questions:

1. Name five positive things about yourself.

2. Name two things that you would like to improve about yourself.

3. What are your plans to improve yourself—spiritually, emotionally, financially, physically, etc.?

New Day
Christian Education, Inc.

Notes

_____

_____

_____

_____

_____

_____

_____

_____

_____

_____

_____

_____

_____

_____

_____

_____

_____

_____

_____

_____

_____

_____

_____

_____

_____

_____

Forgiveness

Activity

Using the notes page answer the following questions:

1. When you think of forgiveness, what comes to mind?
2. Why is it so hard for you to forgive your spouse/ex-spouse?
3. To forgive my spouse/ex-spouse means...
4. To forgive others involved means...
5. To forgive myself means...

Now that you have taken inventory of all sides of your situation, you must repent. True repentance requires you to admit your faults against God and others. You must humble yourself and renounce pride and anything else that would keep you from asking for forgiveness and forgiving others. Ask Him to forgive you and to help you forgive yourself and others, even your spouse.

Forgiveness is a choice, not an emotion. It does not mean that you agree or approve of the wrongs done against you or the wrongs you committed. It means that you release yourself and others of the emotional, mental, physical and spiritual bonds that took place as a result. It is not about anyone else, it is about freeing yourself so that God can be glorified in your life. You don't forget what has occurred but no longer do the chords of bondage have a hold on you.

A prior class participant shared that she called her husband and begin going down a list of things for which she forgave him. She said that it was the most liberating thing that she had done in her process of becoming single. A man shared that he sent an email saying what he forgave his wife for and asking her forgiveness as well, and that freed him. Some have written letters to the ex-spouse (with no

Notes

_____

_____

_____

_____

_____

_____

_____

_____

_____

_____

_____

_____

_____

_____

_____

_____

_____

_____

_____

_____

_____

_____

_____

_____

_____

intention of sending it) and it gave them freedom. Some have contacted others that were involved to ask for forgiveness and to extend forgiveness. Again, it brought healing. Still others just took the matter to God in prayer and left it there, and they were also healed. There is no cookie cutter approach that works for everyone. Also you don't want to put yourself in a position of additional abuse or heartache. Therefore you must prayerfully consider what you need to do for yourself. Read Col. 3:12-13; Prov. 28:13; Ps. 51:17, and pray that God will show you how to forgive and receive forgiveness.

Activity

Using the note pages, answer the following questions:

1. Make a list of things for which you need to forgive your spouse/ex-spouse.
2. Make a list of things for which you need to forgive yourself.
3. Make a list of things for which you need to forgive others who may have been culprits to the failure of your marriage.
4. Ask God to forgive you and help you forgive others, as you read the lists in your prayer to Him. He is faithful and just to forgive you and you can have confidence in prayer. Read 1 John 1:9 and 1 John 5:14-15.

Notes

_____

_____

_____

_____

_____

_____

_____

_____

_____

_____

_____

_____

_____

_____

_____

_____

_____

_____

_____

_____

_____

_____

_____

_____

Singleness (Wholeness)

As stated earlier, in the state of divorce, you are "single-again" (marital status) so you must learn how to be "single" (whole). You are not single from the standpoint of never having been married; hence, the term single-again. The term single-again has a much better connotation than divorced. If you are separated, although you are not divorced, *for the most part* you are also "single-again" and must learn how to be "single" (whole). This does not give you a license to begin dating, as you are not legally divorced and not in a place of wholeness. So what does it mean to be single or whole?

According to Webster's Dictionary, "whole" means...

- Free of wound or injury—unhurt; recovered from a wound or injury—restored; being healed.
- Free of defect or impairment—intact. It means physically sound and healthy—free of disease or deformity.
- Mentally and emotionally sound.

And, "single" is not just unmarried, it is...

- Consisting of a separate unique whole—individual.
- Unbroken and undivided.
- A separate individual person.

According to Steven Jobs (co-founder of Apple), "The benefit of death is you know not to waste life living someone else's choices. Don't let the noise of others' opinions drown out your own inner voice. And most important, have the courage to follow your heart and intuition." We believe this quote is from a "single" or

Notes

_____

_____

_____

_____

_____

_____

_____

_____

_____

_____

_____

_____

_____

_____

_____

_____

_____

_____

_____

_____

_____

_____

_____

_____

_____

whole person. This has to be your attitude and mindset about life. You have to set priorities in life. Your goal must be to make every moment count for something.

You must strive to be single (whole). Herein lies true happiness and fulfillment. Now let's take a look at two main people from the Bible (Adam and Jesus). Take note of the qualities of a single person. According to scripture (Gen. 1:1-26, Gen. 2:4-17) Adam was the first human being. God formed him and breathed life into him and he became a living soul. Prior to forming man, God had already made the heavens and the earth, land and sea, plant life and animal life. He set Adam in the Garden of Eden and gave Adam (subsequently, mankind) dominion over his creation. His responsibility was to dress and keep it. He was running things. God even let Adam name every living creature (Gen. 2:19).

From this you see that Adam was responsible, resourceful, productive, and had an impeccable relationship with God. He knew who he was and whose he was. He was alone but not lonely. Adam was content and fulfilled with him and God alone. As a matter of fact, the Bible does not say that Adam asked for a help meet, but God wanted him to have one (Gen 2:18). Now that's true singleness (wholeness)!

Let's consider Jesus. Although he was divine, God's only begotten son, He was also human. He lived a human existence. He lived a life sold out to pleasing His heavenly father. He was about His Father's business even at an early age (Luke 2:41-50). Because He was human, He experienced the challenges of life just as we do. Read the books of Matthew, Mark, Luke and John for more detail. He cried when his friend died, He was taunted and mocked by the religious people of the day, and even His own people did not really know him. He was betrayed by his close companions, He dreaded going to the cross and asked God if there was another way. He got away to pray and asked his close friends to pray with Him, and so much more. Even so, He was relentless in his pursuit of purpose.

Notes

_____

_____

_____

_____

_____

_____

_____

_____

_____

_____

_____

_____

_____

_____

_____

_____

_____

_____

_____

_____

_____

_____

_____

He knew His purpose and was determined to please God. He did not let His circumstances stop Him. He did not let fear of pain and dread stop Him. He did not let others' opinions stop him. Jesus was determined, courageous, focused, prayerful, and productive. He even died to save the whole world. Surely, that is true singleness (wholeness)!

After looking at two great Biblical examples of singleness (wholeness), this should encourage you to reach for the stars and not to look back. The main thing both had in common was a real relationship with God. You must make Him a priority in your life. If you will allow Him, He will help you move forward. Your present situation is just that. It is where you are now, but it is not the end of you. You can be single and that should be your goal. Allow God to be your focus as you achieve singleness (wholeness). Let God prepare you for what you desire.

A whole person has direction, drive, and focus. They know who they are, where they are going, and have plans of getting there. You must build on YOU before adding someone else to your life. It's all about YOU right now! Just focus on becoming truly single (whole) so that you have something to contribute to any relationship. When you're not whole, you are open to all sorts of trouble and unrest in your life. According to scripture (Prov. 25:28), *"He that hath no rule over his own spirit is like a city that is broken down, and without walls."*

The world began with an individual (single, whole person). Remember being single means you are unhurt, restored, intact, free of deformity, and mentally and emotionally sound, and that you have become a separate unique whole individual—unbroken and undivided. Endeavor to reach a place of completeness and fulfillment with yourself and God. Only then are you truly ready to be married—if that is your desire. You must be single (whole)!

Notes

_____

_____

_____

_____

_____

_____

_____

_____

_____

_____

_____

_____

_____

_____

_____

_____

_____

_____

_____

_____

_____

_____

_____

_____

Activity

Using the notes page, answer the following questions:

Take the time to get to know you. Invest in yourself, in your personal growth and development. Purchase materials that will help you—books, CDs, DVDs, and more. Go to school, take up a new hobby, travel, join a book club, dream again, and more.

1. Who are you?
2. What is your purpose?
3. Name 5 things that you do well. In other words, what are your strengths?
4. Name 3 things that are challenging for you. In other words, what are your weaknesses?
5. What hobbies/pastimes do you enjoy?
6. When was the last time you tried something different and what was it?
7. If money and circumstances were not an issue, what career would you choose?

Notes

_____

_____

_____

_____

_____

_____

_____

_____

_____

_____

_____

_____

_____

_____

_____

_____

_____

_____

_____

_____

_____

_____

Marriage

According to Bishop Rosie S. O'neal, marriage is a union of two free moral agents of the opposite sex who covenant to live with another imperfect person for the rest of their lives in a way that both honors God and brings fulfillment to their lives. The imperfect man and imperfect woman make a covenant before God and to each other. This is a binding commitment naturally and spiritually.

In order for marriage to be as it was designed, you have to learn the Creator's original intentions, so let us take a closer look. Read and study Gen. 2:4-3:6.

From your study, you see that God created man (Adam) and placed him in the Garden of Eden to dress and keep it. He planted trees and commanded him not to eat of "the tree of the knowledge of good and evil" or he would die. Remember from our study so far, Adam was a single (whole) person.

Let's see what it means to be alone versus single. In Gen 2:18 the Bible states, **"And the LORD God said, It is not good that the man should be alone; I will make him an help meet for him."** Accordingly, He said that it is not good for man to be "alone", NOT "single". "Alone" means separated from others or isolated. God knew that man needed relationship on his level. However, everyone needs to be single (a separate unique whole, existing as a distinct entity) for there to be good healthy relationships of any kind.

Interestingly enough, after this statement, God proceeded to make every beast of the field and fowl of the air. He brought them to Adam to see what he would call it, and whatever Adam called it that became the name of it. Even so there was not anything or anyone suitable or compatible with Adam. Then God put Adam in a deep sleep, took one of his ribs and from it made woman. He brought her to Adam just as he had done with every other living creature. Now look at what Adam said in Gen. 2:23, **"And Adam said, this is now bone of my bones, and flesh of my flesh: she shall be called Woman, because she was taken out of Man."**

Notes

_____

_____

_____

_____

_____

_____

_____

_____

_____

_____

_____

_____

_____

_____

_____

_____

_____

_____

_____

_____

_____

_____

_____

_____

_____

_____

After this, God just echoed what Adam said and created the institution of marriage. In Gen. 2:24 God said, **"Therefore shall a man leave his father and his mother, and shall cleave unto his wife: and they shall be one flesh."** In other words, God allowed Adam to make the decision to marry Eve. God gave Adam who he chose as His mate. God just made the presentation, as he had done with all other living creatures. But, Adam made the choice.

"And they were both naked, the man and his wife, and were not ashamed" (Gen. 2:25). They were happy with the choice of being together and were open and free with one another in every way, without feeling ashamed, disappointed or disconcerted in any way. Now this is the ideal marriage relationship.

Now as you read further through Genesis, chapter 3, you will see that there is trouble in paradise. Eve listens to the serpent and eats of the tree that God had told them not to eat of and so did Adam. As a result they lost all that God had provided for them. In the face of their disobedience, blame casting and deception, God still showed grace to them in Gen. 3:21 as he made coats of skins and clothed them. As you can see, they were imperfect people, as they disobeyed God's command. Even so, they stayed together through it all.

It is important that you become whole so that as presentations are made, or relationship opportunities come your way, you can make proper decisions. Without being single first, you run the risk of making unwise decisions and going through failed relationship after failed relationship—a revolving door of heartache and pain.

The Bible states in Prov. 18:22 that **"Whoso findeth a wife findeth a good thing, and obtaineth favour of the LORD."** Again, He is giving man choice. Do not be stuck in the thought that God will send you this perfect mate because there is no such thing—just ask Adam. No one is perfect but Jesus. There are no perfect

Notes

_____
_____
_____
_____
_____
_____
_____
_____
_____
_____
_____
_____
_____
_____
_____
_____
_____
_____
_____
_____
_____
_____
_____
_____
_____

people; however, there are compatible ones. From a filter of true singleness, you have to choose the person that is **most compatible with you now and later**.

Let's summarize what we have learned about marriage:

- **God presented the woman to the man.**
- **God put the institution of marriage together, NOT the people.** "What therefore God hath joined together, let not man put asunder" (Mark 10:9).
- **The people must choose.** God presented Eve to Adam just as He did with the animals. And whatever Adam called them, it was so! Hence, Adam chose Eve as his wife. God established the institution of marriage.
- **God gives you free will.** He does NOT impose on our will. If He doesn't impose on your will to accept Jesus as Savior and Lord, then of course He will not force you to choose a particular person to marry. See 2 Pet. 3:9.

To have a successful marriage, you must go back to Eden where it first began. God instituted marriage; and a single (whole) male and a single (whole) female were joined together. God intended marriage to be permanent.

Don't seek to be married; seek to be "single" in your unmarried state. Only then can you make the proper choice as opportunities are presented.

Activity

Using the notes page, answer the following questions:

1. According to the information provided about Adam, how will you know that you are single (whole)?
2. Are you comfortable in your own skin? In other words, are you happy with YOU?
3. What are you looking for in a life mate?

Notes

_____

_____

_____

_____

_____

_____

_____

_____

_____

_____

_____

_____

_____

_____

_____

_____

_____

_____

_____

_____

_____

_____

_____

_____

PRACTICAL CONSIDERATIONS

Children

When it comes to discussing your divorce or separation with the children, there is no cookie-cutter approach. Be prayerful and seek wisdom from God on the matter. The ideal way to approach the children is with both parents present and sharing with them in a loving way. Although the two of you are at emotional odds with each other, you both love the children and must keep that in the forefront. Ensure that your attitude and behavior is one of mutual respect and love for the children. Be open with the children to the extent that you can be, given the circumstances of the separation or divorce and the age of the children.

If both parents cannot be present, the custodial parent has a duty to openly and loving share with the children (without bias). You do not want to pass judgment or speak ill of the absent parent, as the children will eventually resent you for that. You want the children to have the easiest transition as possible so focus on them. You may want to involve your church youth minister or another leader at your church. This will give you some accountability as you share with your children and engage other resources to help you and the children through this process. This is a very delicate matter and you want to make every effort to handle the ongoing process with care and love. Be a safe place for your children to open up and share their feelings. Often console them in sharing that mommy and daddy are no longer together but both love them and will do the best for them.

Set a meeting to inform the children as soon as possible. As soon as you know the details of living arrangements and visitation, let the children know what is going on. Please avoid sharing on major holidays, birthdays or events, as you do not

Notes

want to forever shed a negative light on a normally happy and joyous occasion. Although you may think you are protecting your children by not sharing, you are really hurting them. Not sharing in a timely manner may cause your children to resent you and distrust you. It can also give them an unhealthy opinion of themselves and their role in the family. You must consistently reassure them that you love them and will continue to care for them. Let them know that the separation or divorce is not their fault nor can they do anything to rectify it. Be honest with them, as much as you can given their age and the circumstances surrounding the matter.

If possible, have the parent who is at fault explain the reason(s) to the children. This way the children can ask questions directly and feel that they have accurate info. Again, the best way is for both parents to speak with the children together. This will also give the children more assurance that the problem is between the parents and not with them. Remember you are doing this for the children. Speak in love and without added emotion. Monitor your children's progress through this difficult time. Allow them to openly express their feelings with you. Involve trusted others as needed to ensure that the children receive what they need to properly adjust to their new life. Do everything you can to keep open lines of communication with the other parent for the sake of the children. The children need to know that both parents love and care for them no matter what.

As you seek God for yourself, involve your children in family prayer and devotion. Let them see how you relate to God and invoke His presence in your daily life.

Notes

_____

_____

_____

_____

_____

_____

_____

_____

_____

_____

_____

_____

_____

_____

_____

_____

_____

_____

_____

_____

_____

_____

_____

Activity

Using the notes page, answer the following questions:

1. How did you or will you share the separation or divorce with your children?
2. How did they respond?
3. What ongoing support are you or others providing them?
4. What are you doing to ensure that they adjust well to the changes?
5. What would or will you do differently now that you have more information?

Notes

_____

_____

_____

_____

_____

_____

_____

_____

_____

_____

_____

_____

_____

_____

_____

_____

_____

_____

_____

_____

_____

_____

_____

_____

_____

Finances

Now that you are single-again, you have most likely gone from a two-income family to one and finances are difficult to manage. You may even have to live off of savings for a while, if there is any. You may have to get a part-time job, work more hours on your current job, train for a new career, have yard sales, ask assistance from family and friends, ask assistance from your spouse or ex-spouse (especially if children are involved), move into a smaller more affordable home, shop at yard sales or thrift stores, eat out less, use coupons, cancel subscriptions, cut back on phone costs, choose low-cost or no-cost entertainment options, or even seek government assistance. Although it may be awkward, the latter part of Jam. 4:2 reads "ye have not, because ye ask not."

Bottom line: your finances will change. The sooner you accept that the better. You will need to plan accordingly and be disciplined to stick to your plan. The good news is if you stick to your plan, in only a few short years, you will have financial stability. It takes work to get to this point, so be patient with yourself and remain consistent.

It may be helpful to have regular family meetings to let the children know what changes will need to be made as a result of the separation or divorce. It may even be helpful to create a family budget together so that everyone will have a clear understanding of where you are and where you are going financially.

The simple math is you either have to make more or spend less, or both. You can do it. There are all sorts of online programs and computer software available to assist you in making a workable budget. It is time for you to get rid of the victim mentality and take charge of your financial present and future. Make an inventory of your gifts, talents and abilities. You will see additional money making options to

Notes

_____
_____
_____
_____
_____
_____
_____
_____
_____
_____
_____
_____
_____
_____
_____
_____
_____
_____
_____
_____
_____
_____
_____
_____
_____

bring more income to your family. For example, if you know how to sew, you may do some alterations on the side. If you are good in math or any other subject matter, you may tutor students in that area of study. If you like to bake, you may sell cakes, pies or cookies during the holidays or for special occasions.

You will have to take steps to get yourself to a place of stability and wholeness in your finances. You need to create and follow a monthly budget, eliminate debts and save money. Get rid of credit cards; eliminate extra stuff like internet, cable or satellite, all phone services except basic service. Shop for less expensive insurance but be sure to maintain life, auto and health insurance. Ask for free or very low-cost financial advice from a trusted adviser. Your church may be a good resource for this service. Seek help and then follow the advice.

Use the following budget percentage guidelines to analyze where you are so you will have an idea of what you need to do to get on track (Taken from Dave Ramsey). To get an accurate picture, you will need to track 4-6 weeks of spending.

Budget – Percentage Guidelines		
Your Budget: Income of $_____/Month		
Charitable giving	10-15%	$_____/month
Housing	25-35%	$_____/month
Utilities	5-10%	$_____/month
Food	5-15%	$_____/month
Transportation	10-15%	$_____/month
Medical	5-10%	$_____/month
Clothing	2-7%	$_____/month
Invest/Savings	5-10%	$_____/month
Debt payments	5-10%	$_____/month
Misc (Personal, Recreation, Life insurance)	5-10%	$_____/month

Notes

_____

_____

_____

_____

_____

_____

_____

_____

_____

_____

_____

_____

_____

_____

_____

_____

_____

_____

_____

_____

_____

_____

Remember to always seek God in everything that you do. Continue to regularly pay tithes and give (Mal. 3:8-12). He will give you wisdom and instruction. According to Deut. 8:18, **"But thou shalt remember the LORD thy God: for it is he that giveth thee power to get wealth, that he may establish his covenant which he sware unto thy fathers, as it is this day."** Trust Him, He is faithful (Prov. 3:5-6)!

Activity

Using the notes page, answer the following questions:

1. Make a list of your gifts, talents, and skills. Even include those things that you think are minor.
2. What are those things that family and friends have always said that you are good at doing?
3. What are some financial adjustments that you have made through this process?
4. How have you either earned more money or spent less, or both?
5. Have you sought financial advice from a trusted financial professional? What has been your experience?
6. Create a family budget. Review and update it monthly, while making necessary adjustments to fully comply.

Notes

_____

_____

_____

_____

_____

_____

_____

_____

_____

_____

_____

_____

_____

_____

_____

_____

_____

_____

_____

_____

_____

_____

_____

_____

Legal Matters

This is where things can get really ugly, really quickly. Unfortunately during this time, you see a side of each other that neither of you even knew existed. It is important to obtain proper legal advice. Divorce can be expensive but it is worth the price to make sure that legal matters are handled appropriately. Shop around and ask trusted others for references. You may also want to check Legal Aid, child welfare services, and other governmental agencies for advice and references.

Although you are emotionally charged, you must remain level headed so that you secure the right attorney for you and that he or she represents your interests adequately. Your lawyer should have experience in family law—at least five years; be professional—competent, resourceful and well-organized; be dedicated to the process of a speedy, equitable and fair resolution; and possess neutrality and impartiality so he or she can give you the best advice at all times.

Share your story with your attorney. Lawyers are trained to obtain the facts that will help in the legal case, not sort through emotional wounds. As much as possible, share the facts as you know them. Let your attorney know your desires for yourself and your children (if you have them). If children are involved, please work on their behalf. Use wisdom in dealing with your spouse or ex-spouse, ensuring that children are not negatively impacted. Remember your attorney works for you so maintain proper perspective throughout the process.

Be sure to handle matters in a Christ-like matter. Always check yourself by asking would God be pleased with your behavior. Be honest with yourself and God. When all is said and done, you want to be able to look at yourself in the mirror without any disdain or disappointment, confident that you have handled matters fittingly.

Notes

_____

_____

_____

_____

_____

_____

_____

_____

_____

_____

_____

_____

_____

_____

_____

_____

_____

_____

_____

_____

_____

_____

_____

Activity

Using the notes page, answer the following questions:

1. Have you sought legal counsel? If so, share your experience. If not, share why.
2. How much can you afford to spend on legal representation?
3. How will you ensure that you consistently receive adequate legal care and responsiveness from your attorney?

Notes

_____

_____

_____

_____

_____

_____

_____

_____

_____

_____

_____

_____

_____

_____

_____

_____

_____

_____

_____

_____

_____

_____

_____

_____

_____

Dating & Remarriage

Once you are truly single (whole) then you may be ready to begin dating. Why is it so important to be whole before dating? If you are not whole, you will make unwise choices and may regret it for the rest of your life. When you are not whole, you look for someone to complete you—to fill the void in you. By doing this, you put the unknowing victim in a place that he or she should not occupy. Only God can fill the voids in your life. Another person should only complement who you are and where you are going. Dating from a perspective of wholeness is safe and efficient. When you know who you are, why you are here, what you are doing, where you are headed, and how you are going to get there, you will not allow anything or anyone to complicate your path. This will give you wisdom in dating.

Dating is a time to get to know people. Yes...people! You need to hang out with more than one person—nothing serious. Keep the conversations light. Sharing personal information too soon can form soul ties. This is where you lose all objectivity and are then led purely by emotions. Pay your own way. No one should even know where you live or how to get to your home at this point. Take things REAL slow.

After some time, you may want to spend more time with one person. Again your first few solo dates should be event driven (ie. Bowling, movies, carnival, and more) and should remain in a public setting. You still should not discuss personal matters. However this is a good time to seek spiritual information. You may say something like, "How did you come to know Jesus as your personal Lord and Savior." If the person has no clue, begins stuttering, or making up stories, that is your opportunity to introduce him or her to someone of the same sex that can minister Christ to him or her. At this point, you need to go in a different direction.

New Day
Christian Education, Inc.

<u>Notes</u>

_____

_____

_____

_____

_____

_____

_____

_____

_____

_____

_____

_____

_____

_____

_____

_____

_____

_____

_____

_____

_____

_____

Do not involve yourself in missionary dating—dating a nonbeliever in an effort to lead them to Christ. It will only lead to disappointment and regret, as you stumble and compromise your standards of holy living.

The next step is dating exclusively. You may decide that one person that you are dating has potential as a life mate and you want to pursue the possibilities. Of course this has to be a mutual decision. Now this is when you need to get to know the person. Explore each others' value system, share personal goals and plans of achieving them, discuss family life and later meet the family, check for compatibility, and more.

If all is going well, then the next step is engagement. Before getting to this point, make sure that you have been honest with yourself. Adhere to red (and all colored) flags, make sure all of your questions or concerns are adequately answered to your satisfaction. You owe this to yourself. You want to do everything possible to avoid another failed marriage. Once you are engaged, find a comprehensive premarital class to attend. Make your attendance and work in this class a priority. As you have experienced, it is so much easier to end the relationship at this stage than to dissolve a marriage.

Of course the last step is remarriage. If this is your goal and what you desire, then congratulations! If you have handled matters in a Godly manner, taken things slow, taken the time to get to know the person, maintained a strong prayer life throughout the process, then you can be confident in God that you are making the right decision for you. Bishop I.V. Hilliard says, "Your mate is the product of your intelligent choice."

Notes

_____

_____

_____

_____

_____

_____

_____

_____

_____

_____

_____

_____

_____

_____

_____

_____

_____

_____

_____

_____

_____

_____

_____

_____

_____

Activity

Using the notes page, answer the following questions:

1. Have you dated since you have been divorced? If you are not divorced, then you should not be dating.
2. Share your dating experiences so far.
3. List 3 positive things you have learned about yourself through the dating process.
4. List 2 negative things you have learned about yourself through the dating process.

Notes

_____

_____

_____

_____

_____

_____

_____

_____

_____

_____

_____

_____

_____

_____

_____

_____

_____

_____

_____

_____

_____

_____

Conclusion

With the divorce rate at around 50%, 1 of 2 married couples you know are likely headed towards ending their relationship. Although God intended and intends for marriage to be permanent, he made provisions for divorce in situations of adultery and abandonment and forgives you for your sins if you divorce for other reasons. Divorce recovery is a grieving process involving stages where you cyclically move forward and backward. Consequently, do not get discouraged if your emotional progress seems slow. On the other hand, forgiveness is not an emotion, but a choice. It is not about the other person, it is about you. Choose to forgive yourself and others thereby, releasing yourself from the emotional and spiritual bondage that unforgiveness breeds.

You are single again. Strive to be complete (whole) in your singleness with a healthy self-image such that if you elect to date you will choose a partner which complements rather than completes you. God created you and you are only complete in him. Don't seek to be married; seek to be "whole" in your unmarried state. Only then can you make the proper choice as dating opportunities are presented.

Do not neglect the business side of divorce. Approach your finances with an awareness of your new reality and budget accordingly. Secure an experienced attorney which will represent your interests effectively during legal matters.

In terms of children, consider your child or children's ages and share on the level of their understanding.

Choose to make better decisions going forward. Hold your head up. Speak life to yourself. Remember your goal is to become single (whole): unhurt, restored, intact, free of deformity, and mentally and emotionally sound, a separate unique

Notes

_____
_____
_____
_____
_____
_____
_____
_____
_____
_____
_____
_____
_____
_____
_____
_____
_____
_____
_____
_____
_____
_____
_____
_____
_____
_____

whole individual—unbroken and undivided. Trust God throughout your process and He will bring you through this season into your New Day.

Appendix A

Relevant Scriptures

Introduction

King James Version (KJV)

Luke 4:18-19

King James Version (KJV)

[18] "The Spirit of the Lord is upon me, because he hath anointed me to preach the gospel to the poor; he hath sent me to heal the brokenhearted, to preach deliverance to the captives, and recovering of sight to the blind, to set at liberty them that are bruised, [19]To preach the acceptable year of the Lord."

Isaiah 61:1-2

King James Version

[1] "The Spirit of the Lord GOD is upon me; because the LORD hath anointed me to preach good tidings unto the meek; he hath sent me to bind up the brokenhearted, to proclaim liberty to the captives, and the opening of the prison to them that are bound; [2]To proclaim the acceptable year of the LORD, and the day of vengeance of our God; to comfort all that mourn;"

New International Version (NIV)

Luke 4:18-19

New International Version (NIV)

[18] "The Spirit of the Lord is on me, because he has anointed me to preach good news to the poor. He has sent me to proclaim freedom for the prisoners and recovery of sight for the blind, to release the oppressed, [19] to proclaim the year of the Lord's favor."

Isaiah 61:1-2

New International Version

[1]"The Spirit of the Sovereign LORD is on me, because the LORD has anointed me to preach good news to the poor. He has sent me to bind up the brokenhearted, to proclaim freedom for the captives and release from darkness for the prisoners,
[2] to proclaim the year of the LORD's favor and the day of vengeance of our God, to comfort all who mourn"

Divorce

Deuteronomy 24:1

King James Version

[1]"When a man hath taken a wife, and married her, and it come to pass that she find no favour in his eyes, because he hath found some uncleanness in her: then let him write her a bill of divorcement, and give it in her hand, and send her out of his house."

Deuteronomy 24:1

New International Version

[1]"If a man marries a woman who becomes displeasing to him because he finds something indecent about her, and he writes her a certificate of divorce, gives it to her and sends her from his house,"

Matthew 19:1-12

King James Version

[1]"And it came to pass, that when Jesus had finished these sayings, he departed from Galilee, and came into the coasts of Judaea beyond Jordan; [2]And great multitudes followed him; and he healed them there. [3]The Pharisees also came unto him, tempting him, and saying unto him, Is it lawful for a man to put away his wife for every cause? [4]And he answered and said unto them, Have ye not read, that he which made them at the beginning made them male and female, [5]And said, For this cause shall a man leave father and mother, and shall cleave to his wife: and they twain shall be one flesh? [6]Wherefore they are no more twain, but one flesh.

Matthew 19:1-12

New International Version

[1]"When Jesus had finished saying these things, he left Galilee and went into the region of Judea to the other side of the Jordan. [2] Large crowds followed him, and he healed them there. [3] Some Pharisees came to him to test him. They asked, "Is it lawful for a man to divorce his wife for any and every reason?"

[4] "Haven't you read," he replied, "that at the beginning the Creator 'made them male and female,' [5] and said, 'For this reason a man will leave his father and mother and be united to his wife, and the two will become one

What therefore God hath joined together, let not man put asunder. [7]They say unto him, Why did Moses then command to give a writing of divorcement, and to put her away? [8]He saith unto them, Moses because of the hardness of your hearts suffered you to put away your wives: but from the beginning it was not so. [9]And I say unto you, Whosoever shall put away his wife, except it be for fornication, and shall marry another, committeth adultery: and whoso marrieth her which is put away doth commit adultery.

[10]His disciples say unto him, If the case of the man be so with his wife, it is not good to marry. [11]But he said unto them, All men cannot receive this saying, save they to whom it is given. [12]For there are some eunuchs, which were so born from their mother's womb: and there are some eunuchs, which were made eunuchs of men: and there be eunuchs, which have made themselves eunuchs for the kingdom of heaven's sake. He that is able to receive it, let him receive it."

flesh'? [6] So they are no longer two, but one. Therefore what God has joined together, let man not separate."[7] "Why then," they asked, "did Moses command that a man give his wife a certificate of divorce and send her away?". [8] Jesus replied, "Moses permitted you to divorce your wives because your hearts were hard. But it was not this way from the beginning. [9] I tell you that anyone who divorces his wife, except for marital unfaithfulness, and marries another woman commits adultery." [10] The disciples said to him, "If this is the situation between a husband and wife, it is better not to marry."

[11] Jesus replied, "Not everyone can accept this word, but only those to whom it has been given. [12] For some are eunuchs because they were born that way; others were made that way by men; and others have renounced marriage because of the kingdom of heaven. The one who can accept this should accept it."

Malachi 2:14-16

King James Version

¹⁴"Yet ye say, Wherefore? Because the LORD hath been witness between thee and the wife of thy youth, against whom thou hast dealt treacherously: yet is she thy companion, and the wife of thy covenant.

¹⁵And did not he make one? Yet had he the residue of the spirit. And wherefore one? That he might seek a godly seed. Therefore take heed to your spirit, and let none deal treacherously against the wife of his youth.

¹⁶For the LORD, the God of Israel, saith that he hateth putting away: for one covereth violence with his garment, saith the LORD of hosts: therefore take heed to your spirit, that ye deal not treacherously."

Malachi 2:14-16

New International Version

¹⁴"You ask, "Why?" It is because the LORD is acting as the witness between you and the wife of your youth, because you have broken faith with her, though she is your partner, the wife of your marriage covenant.

¹⁵ Has not the LORD made them one? In flesh and spirit they are his. And why one?Because he was seeking godly offspring. So guard yourself in your spirit, and do not break faith with the wife of your youth.

¹⁶ "I hate divorce," says the LORD God of Israel, "and I hate a man's covering himself with violence as well as with his garment," says the LORD Almighty. So guard yourself in your spirit, and do not break faith."

Matthew 19:8

King James Version

[8] He saith unto them, Moses because of the hardness of your hearts suffered you to put away your wives: but from the beginning it was not so.

Matthew 5:31-32

King James Version

[31] "It hath been said, Whosoever shall put away his wife, let him give her a writing of divorcement: [32]But I say unto you, That whosoever shall put away his wife, saving for the cause of fornication, causeth her to commit adultery: and whosoever shall marry her that is divorced committeth adultery."

Matthew 19:3-11

King James Version

[3] The Pharisees also came unto him, tempting him, and saying unto him, Is it lawful for a man to put away his wife for every cause?

[4] And he answered and said unto them, Have ye not read, that he which made them at the beginning made them male and female.

Matthew 19:8

King James Version

[8] Jesus replied, "Moses permitted you to divorce your wives because your hearts were hard. But it was not this way from the beginning.

Matthew 5:31-32

New International Version

[31] "It has been said, 'Anyone who divorces his wife must give her a certificate of divorce.[32] But I tell you that anyone who divorces his wife, except for marital unfaithfulness, causes her to become an adulteress, and anyone who marries the divorced woman commits adultery."

Matthew 19:3-11

New International Version

[3] Some Pharisees came to him to test him. They asked, "Is it lawful for a man to divorce his wife for any and every reason?"

[4] "Haven't you read," he replied, "that at the beginning the Creator 'made them male and female,'

[5] And said, For this cause shall a man leave father and mother, and shall cleave to his wife: and they twain shall be one flesh?

[6] Wherefore they are no more twain, but one flesh. What therefore God hath joined together, let not man put asunder.

[7] They say unto him, Why did Moses then command to give a writing of divorcement, and to put her away?

[8] He saith unto them, Moses because of the hardness of your hearts suffered you to put away your wives: but from the beginning it was not so.

[9] And I say unto you, Whosoever shall put away his wife, except it be for fornication, and shall marry another, committeth adultery: and whoso marrieth her which is put away doth commit adultery.

[10] His disciples say unto him, If the case of the man be so with his wife, it is not good to marry.

[11] But he said unto them, All men cannot receive this saying, save they to whom it is given.

[5] and said, 'For this reason a man will leave his father and mother and be united to his wife, and the two will become one flesh'? [6] So they are no longer two, but one flesh. Therefore what God has joined together, let no one separate."

[7] "Why then," they asked, "did Moses command that a man give his wife a certificate of divorce and send her away?"

[8] Jesus replied, "Moses permitted you to divorce your wives because your hearts were hard. But it was not this way from the beginning. [9] I tell you that anyone who divorces his wife, except for sexual immorality, and marries another woman commits adultery."

[10] The disciples said to him, "If this is the situation between a husband and wife, it is better not to marry."

[11] Jesus replied, "Not everyone can accept this word, but only those to whom it has been given."

1 Corinthians 7:10-17

King James Version

[10]"And unto the married I command, yet not I, but the Lord, Let not the wife depart from her husband: [11]But and if she depart, let her remain unmarried or be reconciled to her husband: and let not the husband put away his wife.[12]But to the rest speak I, not the Lord: If any brother hath a wife that believeth not, and she be pleased to dwell with him, let him not put her away.

[13]And the woman which hath an husband that believeth not, and if he be pleased to dwell with her, let her not leave him. [14]For the unbelieving husband is sanctified by the wife, and the unbelieving wife is sanctified by the husband: else were your children unclean; but now are they holy.[15]But if the unbelieving depart, let him depart. A brother or a sister is not under bondage in such cases: but God hath called us to peace.

[16]For what knowest thou, O wife, whether thou shalt save thy husband? or how knowest thou, O man, whether thou shalt save thy wife?[17]But as God hath distributed to every man, as the Lord hath called every one, so let him walk. And so ordain I in all churches."

1 Corinthians 7:10-17

New International Version

[10]"To the married I give this command (not I, but the Lord): A wife must not separate from her husband. [11] But if she does, she must remain unmarried or else be reconciled to her husband. And a husband must not divorce his wife.

[12] To the rest I say this (I, not the Lord): If any brother has a wife who is not a believer and she is willing to live with him, he must not divorce her. [13] And if a woman has a husband who is not a believer and he is willing to live with her, she must not divorce him. [14] For the unbelieving husband has been sanctified through his wife, and the unbelieving wife has been sanctified through her believing husband. Otherwise your children would be unclean, but as it is, they are holy.

[15] But if the unbeliever leaves, let him do so. A believing man or woman is not bound in such circumstances; God has called us to live in peace. [16] How do you know, wife, whether you will save your husband? Or, how do you know, husband, whether you will save your wife? [17] Nevertheless, each one should retain the place in life that the Lord assigned to him and to which God has called him. This is the rule I lay down in all the churches."

1 John 1:9

King James Version

[9]"If we confess our sins, he is faithful and just to forgive us our sins, and to cleanse us from all unrighteousness."

1 John 1:9

New International Version

[9]"If we confess our sins, he is faithful and just and will forgive us our sins and purify us from all unrighteousness."

Emotions and Self-image

Romans 8:37

King James Version

[37]"Nay, in all these things we are more than conquerors through him that loved us."

Romans 8:37

New International Version

[37]"No, in all these things we are more than conquerors through him who loved us."

Zechariah 2:8

King James Version

[8]"For thus saith the LORD of hosts; After the glory hath he sent me unto the nations which spoiled you: for he that toucheth you toucheth the apple of his eye."

Zechariah 2:8

New International Version

[8]"For this is what the LORD Almighty says: "After he has honored me and has sent me against the nations that have plundered you—for whoever touches you touches the apple of his eye"

Psalm 17:8

King James Version

8 "Keep me as the apple of the eye, hide me under the shadow of thy wings,"

Psalm 17:8

New International Version

8"Keep me as the apple of your eye; hide me in the shadow of your wings"

Psalm 139:14

King James Version

14 "I will praise thee; for I am fearfully and wonderfully made: marvellous are thy works; and that my soul knoweth right well."

Psalm 139:14

New International Version

14"I praise you because I am fearfully and wonderfully made;
   your works are wonderful, I know that full well."

Luke 12:7

King James Version

7 "But even the very hairs of your head are all numbered. Fear not therefore: ye are of more value than many sparrows."

Luke 12:7

New International Version

7 "Indeed, the very hairs of your head are all numbered. Don't be afraid; you are worth more than many sparrows."

Proverbs 18:21

King James Version

[21]"Death and life are in the power of the tongue: and they that love it shall eat the fruit thereof."

Proverbs 18:21

New International Version

[21]"The tongue has the power of life and death, and those who love it will eat its fruit."

Matthew 22:37-40

King James Version

[37]"Jesus said unto him, Thou shalt love the Lord thy God with all thy heart, and with all thy soul, and with your soul and with all your mind." [38] This is the first and greatest commandment. [39] And the second is like it: 'Love your neighbor as yourself.' [40] All the Law and the Prophets hang on these two commandments."

Matthew 22:37-40

New International Version

[37]"Jesus replied: 'Love the Lord your God with all your heart and with all all thy mind." [38]This is the first and great commandment. [39]And the second is like unto it, Thou shalt love thy neighbour as thyself. [40]On these two commandments hang all the law and the prophets."

Genesis 1:31

King James Version

[31]"And God saw every thing that he had made, and, behold, it was very good. And the evening and the morning were the sixth day."

Genesis 1:31

New International Version

[31]"God saw all that he had made, and it was very good. And there was evening, and there was morning—the sixth day."

Forgiveness

Colossians 3:12-13

King James Version

[12]"Put on therefore, as the elect of God, holy and beloved, bowels of mercies, kindness, humbleness of mind, meekness, longsuffering;"

[13]Forbearing one another, and forgiving one another, if any man have a quarrel against any: even as Christ forgave you, so also do ye.

Colossians 3:12-13

New International Version

[12]"Therefore, as God's chosen people, holy and dearly loved, clothe yourselves with compassion, kindness, humility, gentleness and patience. [13] Bear with each other and forgive whatever grievances you may have against one another. Forgive as the Lord forgave you."

Proverbs 28:13

King James Version

[13] "He that covereth his sins shall not prosper: but whoso confesseth and forsaketh them shall have mercy."

Proverbs 28:13

New International Version

[13] "He who conceals his sins does not prosper, but whoever confesses and renounces them finds mercy."

Psalm 51:17

King James Version

[17] "The sacrifices of God are a broken spirit: a broken and a contrite heart, O God, thou wilt not despise."

Psalm 51:17

New International Version

[17] "The sacrifices of God are a broken spirit; a broken and contrite heart,
     O God, you will not despise."

1 John 1:9

King James Version

[9] If we confess our sins, he is faithful and just to forgive us our sins, and to cleanse us from all unrighteousness.

1 John 1:9

New International Version

[9] If we confess our sins, he is faithful and just and will forgive us our sins and purify us from all unrighteousness.

1 John 5:14-15

King James Version

[14] "And this is the confidence that we have in him, that, if we ask any thing according to his will, he heareth us: [15] And if we know that he hear us, whatsoever we ask, we know that we have the petitions that we desired of him."

1 John 5:14-15

New International Version

[14]"This is the confidence we have in approaching God: that if we ask anything according to his will, he hears us. [15] And if we know that he hears us—whatever we ask—we know that we have what we asked of him.

Singleness (Wholeness)

Genesis 1:1-26

King James Version

[1]In the beginning God created the heaven and the earth. [2]And the earth was without form, and void; and darkness was upon the face of the deep. And the Spirit of God moved upon the face of the waters. [3]And God said, Let there be light: and there was light.

Genesis 1:1-26

New International Version

[1]"In the beginning God created the heavens and the earth.[2] Now the earth was formless and empty, darkness was over the surface of the deep, and the Spirit of God was hovering over the waters. [3] And God said, "Let there be light," and there was light.

⁴And God saw the light, that it was good: and God divided the light from the darkness.⁵And God called the light Day, and the darkness he called Night. And the evening and the morning were the first day. ⁶And God said, Let there be a firmament in the midst of the waters, and let it divide the waters from the waters. ⁷And God made the firmament, and divided the waters which were under the firmament from the waters which were above the firmament: and it was so. ⁸And God called the firmament Heaven. And the evening and the morning were the second day. ⁹And God said, Let the waters under the heaven be gathered together unto one place, and let the dry land appear: and it was so. ¹⁰And God called the dry land Earth; and the gathering together of the waters called he Seas: and God saw that it was good.

¹⁷And God set them in the firmament of the heaven to give light upon the earth, ¹⁸And to rule over the day and over the night, and to divide the light from the darkness: and God saw that it was good. ¹⁹And the evening and the morning were the fourth day.

⁴ God saw that the light was good, and he separated the light from the darkness. ⁵ God called the light "day," and the darkness he called "night." And there was evening, and there was morning— the first day. ⁶ And God said, "Let there be an expanse between the waters to separate water from water." ⁷ So God made the expanse and separated the water under the expanse from the water above it. And it was so. ⁸ God called the expanse "sky." And there was evening, and there was morning—the second day. ⁹ And God said, "Let the water under the sky be gathered to one place, and let dry ground appear." And it was so. ¹⁰ God called the dry ground "land," and the gathered waters he called "seas." And God saw that it was good.

¹¹ Then God said, "Let the land produce vegetation: seed-bearing plants and trees on the land that bear fruit with seed in it, according to their various kinds." And it was so.

New Day
Christian Education, Inc.

[20]And God said, Let the waters bring forth abundantly the moving creature that hath life, and fowl that may fly above the earth in the open firmament of heaven. [21]And God created great whales, and every living creature that moveth, which the waters brought forth abundantly, after their kind, and every winged fowl after his kind: and God saw that it was good. [22]And God blessed them, saying, Be fruitful, and multiply, and fill the waters in the seas, and let fowl multiply in the earth. [23]And the evening and the morning were the fifth day. [24]And God said, Let the earth bring forth the living creature after his kind, cattle, and creeping thing, and beast of the earth after his kind: and it was so. [25]And God made the beast of the earth after his kind, and cattle after their kind, and every thing that creepeth upon the earth after his kind: and God saw that it was good. [26]And God said, Let us make man in our image, after our likeness: and let them have dominion over the fish of the sea, and over the fowl of the air, and over the cattle, and over all the earth, and over every creeping thing that creepeth upon the earth."

[12] The land produced vegetation: plants bearing seed according to their kinds and trees bearing fruit with seed in it according to their kinds. And God saw that it was good. [13] And there was evening, and there was morning—the third day. [14] And God said, "Let there be lights in the expanse of the sky to separate the day from the night, and let them serve as signs to mark seasons and days and years, [15] and let them be lights in the expanse of the sky to give light on the earth." And it was so. [16] God made two great lights—the greater light to govern the day and the lesser light to govern the night. He also made the stars. [17] God set them in the expanse of the sky to give light on the earth, [18] to govern the day and the night, and to separate light from darkness. And God saw that it was good. [19] And there was evening, and there was morning—the fourth day. [20] And God said, "Let the water teem with living creatures, and let birds fly above the earth across the expanse of the sky."

[21] So God created the great creatures of the sea and every living and moving thing with which the water teems, according to their kinds, and every winged bird according to its kind. And God saw that it was good. [22] God blessed them and said, "Be fruitful and increase in number and fill the water in the seas, and let the birds increase on the earth." [23] And there was evening, and there was morning—the fifth day. [24] And God said, "Let the land produce living creatures according to their kinds: livestock, creatures that move along the ground, and wild animals, each according to its kind." And it was so. [25] God made the wild animals according to their kinds, the livestock according to their kinds, and all the creatures that move along the ground according to their kinds. And God saw that it was good.

[26] Then God said, "Let us make man in our image, in our likeness, and let them rule over the fish of the sea and the birds of the air, over the livestock, over all the earth, and over all the creatures that move along the ground."

Genesis 2:4-17

King James Version

⁴These are the generations of the heavens and of the earth when they were created, in the day that the LORD God made the earth and the heavens, ⁵And every plant of the field before it was in the earth, and every herb of the field before it grew: for the LORD God had not caused it to rain upon the earth, and there was not a man to till the ground. ⁶But there went up a mist from the earth, and watered the whole face of the ground. ⁷And the LORD God formed man of the dust of the ground, and breathed into his nostrils the breath of life; and man became a living soul.⁸And the LORD God planted a garden eastward in Eden; and there he put the man whom he had formed. ⁹And out of the ground made the LORD God to grow every tree that is pleasant to the sight, and good for food; the tree of life also in the midst of the garden, and the tree of knowledge of good and evil.

Genesis 2:4-17

New International Version

⁴ This is the account of the heavens and the earth when they were created. When the LORD God made the earth and the heavens— ⁵ and no shrub of the field had yet appeared on the earthand no plant of the field had yet sprung up, for the LORD God had not sent rain on the earth and there was no man to work the ground, ⁶ but streams came up from the earth and watered the whole surface of the ground— ⁷ the LORD God formed the man from the dust of the ground and breathed into his nostrils the breath of life, and the man became a living being. ⁸ Now the LORD God had planted a garden in the east, in Eden; and there he put the man he had formed. ⁹ And the LORD God made all kinds of trees grow out of the ground—trees that were pleasing to the eye and good for food. In the middle of the garden were the tree of life and the tree of the knowledge of good and evil.

¹⁰And a river went out of Eden to water the garden; and from thence it was parted, and became into four heads.

¹¹The name of the first is Pison: that is it which compasseth the whole land of Havilah, where there is gold; ¹²And the gold of that land is good: there is bdellium and the onyx stone. ¹³And the name of the second river is Gihon: the same is it that compasseth the whole land of Ethiopia. ¹⁴And the name of the third river is Hiddekel: that is it which goeth toward the east of Assyria. And the fourth river is Euphrates. ¹⁵And the LORD God took the man, and put him into the garden of Eden to dress it and to keep it.¹⁶And the LORD God commanded the man, saying, Of every tree of the garden thou mayest freely eat: ¹⁷But of the tree of the knowledge of good and evil, thou shalt not eat of it: for in the day that thou eatest thereof thou shalt surely die.

¹⁰ A river watering the garden flowed from Eden; from there it was separated into four headwaters.

¹¹ The name of the first is the Pishon; it winds through the entire land of Havilah, where there is gold. ¹² (The gold of that land is good; aromatic resin and onyx are also there.) ¹³The name of the second river is the Gihon; it winds through the entire land of Cush. ¹⁴ The name of the third river is the Tigris; it runs along the east side of Asshur. And the fourth river is the Euphrates. ¹⁵ The LORD God took the man and put him in the Garden of Eden to work it and take care of it. ¹⁶ And the LORD God commanded the man, "You are free to eat from any tree in the garden; ¹⁷ but you must not eat from the tree of the knowledge of good and evil, for when you eat of it you will surely die."

Genesis 2:19

King James Version

[19] "And out of the ground the LORD God formed every beast of the field, and every fowl of the air; and brought them unto Adam to see what he would call them: and whatsoever Adam called every living creature, that was the name thereof."

Genesis 2:19

New International Version

[19] "Now the LORD God had formed out of the ground all the beasts of the field and all the birds of the air. He brought them to the man to see what he would name them; and whatever the man called each living creature, that was its name

Genesis 2:18

King James Version

[18] "And the LORD God said, It is not good that the man should be alone; I will make him an help meet for him."

Genesis 2:18

New International Version

[18] "The LORD God said, "It is not good for the man to be alone. I will make a helper suitable for him."

Luke 2:41-50

King James Version

[41] "Now his parents went to Jerusalem every year at the feast of the passover. [42] And when he was twelve years old, they went up to Jerusalem after the custom of the feast.

Luke 2:41-50

New International Version

[41] "Every year his parents went to Jerusalem for the Feast of the Passover. [42] When he was twelve years old, they went up to the Feast, according to the custom.

⁴³ And when they had fulfilled the days, as they returned, the child Jesus tarried behind in Jerusalem; and Joseph and his mother knew not of it acquaintance. ⁴⁴ But they, supposing him to have been in the company, went a day's journey; and they sought him among their kinsfolk and ⁴⁵ And when they found him not, they turned back again to Jerusalem, seeking him. ⁴⁶ And it came to pass, that after three days they found him in the temple, sitting in the midst of the doctors, both hearing them, and asking them questions. ⁴⁷ And all that heard him were astonished at his understanding and answers. ⁴⁸ And when they saw him, they were amazed: and his mother said unto him, Son, why hast thou thus dealt with us? behold, thy father and I have sought thee sorrowing. ⁴⁹ And he said unto them, How is it that ye sought me? wist ye not that I must be about my Father's business? ⁵⁰ And they understood not the saying which he spake unto them.

⁴³ After the Feast was over, while his parents were returning home, the boy Jesus stayed behind in Jerusalem, but they were unaware of it. ⁴⁴ Thinking he was in their company, they traveled on for a day. Then they began looking for him among their relatives and friends. ⁴⁵ When they did not find him, they went back to Jerusalem to look for him.

⁴⁶ After three days they found him in the temple courts, sitting among the teachers, listening to them and asking them questions. ⁴⁷ Everyone who heard him was amazed at his understanding and his answers. ⁴⁸ When his parents saw him, they were astonished. His mother said to him, "Son, why have you treated us like this? Your father and I have been anxiously searching for you." ⁴⁹ "Why were you searching for me?" he asked. "Didn't you know I had to be in my Father's house?" ⁵⁰ But they did not understand what he was saying to them."

Proverbs 25:28

King James Version

²⁸"He that hath no rule over his own spirit is like a city that is broken down, and without walls."

Proverbs 25:28

New International Version

²⁸"Like a city whose walls are broken down is a man who lacks self-control."

Marriage

Genesis 2:4 - 3:6

King James Version

⁴These are the generations of the heavens and of the earth when they were created, in the day that the LORD God made the earth and the heavens, ⁵And every plant of the field before it was in the earth, and every herb of the field before it grew: for the LORD God had not caused it to rain upon the earth, and there was not a man to till the ground. ⁶But there went up a mist from the earth, and watered the whole face of the ground. ⁷And the LORD God formed man of the dust of the ground, and breathed into his nostrils the breath of life; and man became a living soul.

Genesis 2:4 - 3:6

New International Version

⁴ This is the account of the heavens and the earth when they were created. When the LORD God made the earth and the heavens— ⁵ and no shrub of the field had yet appeared on the earth and no plant of the field had yet sprung up, for the LORD God had not sent rain on the earth and there was no man to work the ground, ⁶ but streams came up from the earth and watered the whole surface of the ground— ⁷ the LORD God formed the man from the dust of the ground and breathed into his nostrils the breath of life, and the man became a living being.

[8]And the LORD God planted a garden eastward in Eden; and there he put the man whom he had formed. [9]And out of the ground made the LORD God to grow every tree that is pleasant to the sight, and good for food; the tree of life also in the midst of the garden, and the tree of knowledge of good and evil.[10]And a river went out of Eden to water the garden; and from thence it was parted, and became into four heads.[11]The name of the first is Pison: that is it which compasseth the whole land of Havilah, where there is gold;[12]And the gold of that land is good: there is bdellium and the onyx stone. [13]And the name of the second river is Gihon: the same is it that compasseth the whole land of Ethiopia. [14]And the name of the third river is Hiddekel: that is it which goeth toward the east of Assyria. And the fourth river is Euphrates.[15]And the LORD God took the man, and put him into the garden of Eden to dress it and to keep it.[16]And the LORD God commanded the man, saying, Of every tree of the garden thou mayest freely eat:

[8] Now the LORD God had planted a garden in the east, in Eden; and there he put the man he had formed. [9] And the LORD God made all kinds of trees grow out of the ground—trees that were pleasing to the eye and good for food. In the middle of the garden were the tree of life and the tree of the knowledge of good and evil. [10] A river watering the garden flowed from Eden; from there it was separated into four headwaters.[11] The name of the first is the Pishon; it winds through the entire land of Havilah, where there is gold. [12] (The gold of that land is good; aromatic resin and onyx are also there.) [13]The name of the second river is the Gihon; it winds through the entire land of Cush. [14] The name of the third river is the Tigris; it runs along the east side of Asshur. And the fourth river is the Euphrates. [15] The LORD God took the man and put him in the Garden of Eden to work it and take care of it.

[17]But of the tree of the knowledge of good and evil, thou shalt not eat of it: for in the day that thou eatest thereof thou shalt surely die. [18]And the LORD God said, It is not good that the man should be alone; I will make him an help meet for him.[19]And out of the ground the LORD God formed every beast of the field, and every fowl of the air; and brought them unto Adam to see what he would call them: and whatsoever Adam called every living creature, that was the name thereof. [20]And Adam gave names to all cattle, and to the fowl of the air, and to every beast of the field; but for Adam there was not found an help meet for him. [21]And the LORD God caused a deep sleep to fall upon Adam, and he slept: and he took one of his ribs, and closed up the flesh instead thereof; [22]And the rib, which the LORD God had taken from man, made he a woman, and brought her unto the man

[16] And the LORD God commanded the man, "You are free to eat from any tree in the garden; [17] but you must not eat from the tree of the knowledge of good and evil, for when you eat of it you will surely die." [18] The LORD God said, "It is not good for the man to be alone. I will make a helper suitable for him." [19] Now the LORD God had formed out of the ground all the beasts of the field and all the birds of the air. He brought them to the man to see what he would name them; and whatever the man called each living creature, that was its name. [20] So the man gave names to all the livestock, the birds of the air and all the beasts of the field. But for Adam no suitable helper was found. [21] So the LORD God caused the man to fall into a deep sleep; and while he was sleeping, he took one of the man's ribs and closed up the place with flesh.

[23]And Adam said, This is now bone of my bones, and flesh of my flesh: she shall be called Woman, because she was taken out of Man.[24]Therefore shall a man leave his father and his mother, and shall cleave unto his wife: and they shall be one flesh.[25]And they were both naked, the man and his wife, and were not ashamed.

Chapter 3 Now the serpent was more subtil than any beast of the field which the LORD God had made. And he said unto the woman, Yea, hath God said, Ye shall not eat of every tree of the garden? [2] And the woman said unto the serpent, We may eat of the fruit of the trees of the garden: [3] But of the fruit of the tree which is in the midst of the garden, God hath said, Ye shall not eat of it, neither shall ye touch it, lest ye die. [4] And the serpent said unto the woman, Ye shall not surely die: [5] For God doth know that in the day ye eat thereof, then your eyes shall be opened, and ye shall be as gods, knowing good and evil. [6] And when the woman saw that the tree was good for food, and that it was pleasant to the eyes, and a tree to be desired to make one wise, she took of the fruit thereof, and did eat, and gave also unto her husband with her; and he did eat.

[22] Then the LORD God made a woman from the rib he had taken out of the man, and he brought her to the man. [23] The man said, "This is now bone of my bones and flesh of my flesh; she shall be called woman,'for she was taken out of man." [24] For this reason a man will leave his father and mother and be united to his wife, and they will become one flesh. [25] The man and his wife were both naked, and they felt no shame.

Chapter 3 Now the serpent was more crafty than any of the wild animals the LORD God had made. He said to the woman, "Did God really say, 'You must not eat from any tree in the garden'?" [2] The woman said to the serpent, "We may eat fruit from the trees in the garden, [3] but God did say, 'You must not eat fruit from the tree that is in the middle of the garden, and you must not touch it, or you will die.'" [4] "You will not surely die," the serpent said to the woman. [5] "For God knows that when you eat of it your eyes will be opened, and you will be like God, knowing good and evil." [6] When the woman saw that the fruit of the tree was good for food and pleasing to the eye, and also desirable for gaining wisdom, she took some and ate it. She also gave some to her husband, who was with her, and he ate it.

Genesis 2:18

King James Version

[18] And the LORD God said, It is not good that the man should be alone; I will make him an help meet for him.

Genesis 2:18

New International Version

[18] The LORD God said, "It is not good for the man to be alone. I will make a helper suitable for him."

Genesis 2:23

King James Version

[23] And Adam said, This is now bone of my bones, and flesh of my flesh: she shall be called Woman, because she was taken out of Man.

Genesis 2:23

New International Version

[23] The man said,"This is now bone of my bones and flesh of my flesh; she shall be called 'woman,'for she was taken out of man. "

Genesis 2:24

King James Version

[24] Therefore shall a man leave his father and his mother, and shall cleave unto his wife: and they shall be one flesh.

Genesis 2:24

New International Version

[24] That is why a man leaves his father and mother and is united to his wife, and they become one flesh.

Genesis 2:25

King James Version

[25] And they were both naked, the man and his wife, and were not ashamed.

Genesis 2:25

New International Version

[25] The man and his wife were both naked, and they felt no shame.

Genesis 3:1-6

King James Version

¹Now the serpent was more subtil than any beast of the field which the LORD God had made. And he said unto the woman, Yea, hath God said, Ye shall not eat of every tree of the garden? ²And the woman said unto the serpent, We may eat of the fruit of the trees of the garden: ³But of the fruit of the tree which is in the midst of the garden, God hath said, Ye shall not eat of it, neither shall ye touch it, lest ye die. ⁴And the serpent said unto the woman, Ye shall not surely die: ⁵For God doth know that in the day ye eat thereof, then your eyes shall be opened, and ye shall be as gods, knowing good and evil. ⁶And when the woman saw that the tree was good for food, and that it was pleasant to the eyes, and a tree to be desired to make one wise, she took of the fruit thereof, and did eat, and gave also unto her husband with her; and he did eat.

Genesis 3:21

King James Version

²¹ Unto Adam also and to his wife did the LORD God make coats of skins, and clothed them.

Genesis 3:1-6

New International Version

¹"Now the serpent was more crafty than any of the wild animals the LORD God had made. He said to the woman, "Did God really say, 'You must not eat from any tree in the garden'?" ² The woman said to the serpent, "We may eat fruit from the trees in the garden, ³ but God did say, 'You must not eat fruit from the tree that is in the middle of the garden, and you must not touch it, or you will die.' ⁴ "You will not surely die," the serpent said to the woman. ⁵ "For God knows that when you eat of it your eyes will be opened, and you will be like God, knowing good and evil."⁶ When the woman saw that the fruit of the tree was good for food and pleasing to the eye, and also desirable for gaining wisdom, she took some and ate it. She also gave some to her husband, who was with her, and he ate it.

Genesis 3:21

New International Version

²¹ The LORD God made garments of skin for Adam and his wife and clothed them.

Proverbs 18:22

King James Version

²²"Whoso findeth a wife findeth a good thing, and obtaineth favour of the LORD."

Proverbs 18:22

New International Version

²²"He who finds a wife finds what is goodand receives favor from the LORD".

Mark 10:9

King James Version

⁹ What therefore God hath joined together, let not man put asunder.

Mark 10:9

New International Version

⁹ Therefore what God has joined together, let no one separate."

2 Peter 3:9

King James Version

⁹"The Lord is not slack concerning his promise, as some men count slackness; but is longsuffering to us-ward, not willing that any should perish, but that all should come to repentance."

2 Peter 3:9

New International Version

⁹"The Lord is not slow in keeping his promise, as some understand slowness. He is patient with you, not wanting anyone to perish, but everyone to come to repentance."

PRACTICAL CONSIDERATIONS

Finances

James 4:2

King James Version

[2] "Ye lust, and have not: ye kill, and desire to have, and cannot obtain: ye fight and war, yet ye have not, because ye ask not."

James 4:2

New International Version

[2]"You want something but don't get it. You kill and covet, but you cannot have what you want. You quarrel and fight. You do not have, because you do not ask God."

Malachi 3:8-12

King James Version

[8]"Will a man rob God? Yet ye have robbed me. But ye say, Wherein have we robbed thee? In tithes and offerings.[9]Ye are cursed with a curse: for ye have robbed me, even this whole nation. [10]Bring ye all the tithes into the storehouse, that there may be meat in mine house, and prove me now herewith, saith the LORD of hosts, if I will not open you the windows of heaven, and pour you out a blessing, that there shall not be room enough to receive it. [11]And I will rebuke the devourer for your sakes, and he shall not destroy the fruits of your ground; neither shall your vine cast her fruit before the time

Malachi 3:8-12

New International Version

[8] "Will a man rob God? Yet you rob me. "But you ask, 'How do we rob you?' "In tithes and offerings.[9] You are under a curse—the whole nation of you—because you are robbing me. [10] Bring the whole tithe into the storehouse, that there may be food in my house. Test me in this," says the LORD Almighty, "and see if I will not throw open the floodgates of heaven and pour out so much blessing that you will not have room enough for it.

[11] I will prevent pests from devouring your crops, and the vines in your fields will not cast their fruit," says

in the field, saith the LORD of hosts. [12]And all nations shall call you blessed: for ye shall be a delightsome land, saith the LORD of hosts."

the LORD Almighty. [12] "Then all the nations will call you blessed, for yours will be a delightful land," says the LORD Almight

Deuteronomy 8:18

King James Version

[18]"But thou shalt remember the LORD thy God: for it is he that giveth thee power to get wealth, that he may establish his covenant which he sware unto thy fathers, as it is this day."

Deuteronomy 8:18

New International Version

[18]"But remember the LORD your God, for it is he who gives you the ability to produce wealth, and so confirms his covenant, which he swore to your forefathers, as it is today."

Proverbs 3:5-6

King James Version

[5]"Trust in the LORD with all thine heart; and lean not unto thine own understanding.[6]In all thy ways acknowledge him, and he shall direct thy paths".

Proverbs 3:5-6

New International Version

[5]"Trust in the LORD with all your heart and lean not on your own understanding;
[6] in all your ways acknowledge him, and he will make your paths straight."

Appendix B

Salvation Opportunity

Give your life to Jesus Christ TODAY!

Jesus desires to be your Savior and lord. Savior means that He keeps you from destruction and eternal damnation. Lord means He rules and reigns in your heart and life. Give Him your concerns and cares and let Him bring fulfillment to your life. Let Jesus remind you of your purpose for being here so that you can do all that you were sent to do and be for the Kingdom of God.

Pray this prayer:

Father, in the name of Jesus, I come to you today with a heart of repentance and gratitude for all that you have done for me. I believe that you sent your son Jesus to die on the cross, be buried, and rise again just for me. And He did just that. Jesus, I accept what You did for me. I ask that You will come into my heart and change me from the inside out. I repent of all my sins and choose to follow You. Help me to live this new life and draw others to your saving grace. Thank you for receiving me into Your family. In Jesus' name I pray...AMEN!

Signature_____

Date_____

Appendix C

Prayer Request

[We encourage you to make copies of this page for future use.]

We know our God to be a prayer answerer. He is ever mindful of us. He said that He'd never leave us nor forsake us (Heb. 13:5). His word tells us "And all things, whatsoever ye shall ask in prayer, believing, ye shall receive" (Matt. 21:22). Also, "The effectual fervent prayer of a righteous man availeth much" (Jam 5:16). God's word tells us, "Be careful for nothing; but in every thing by prayer and supplication with thanksgiving let your requests be made known unto God" (Phil. 4:6).Knowing this, write your prayer request(s) in the space provided so that we can agree in prayer with you according to Matt. 18:18-20...

[18]Verily I say unto you, Whatsoever ye shall bind on earth shall be bound in heaven: and whatsoever ye shall loose on earth shall be loosed in heaven.

[19]Again I say unto you, That if two of you shall agree on earth as touching any thing that they shall ask, it shall be done for them of my Father which is in heaven.

[20]For where two or three are gathered together in my name, there am I in the midst of them.

Date _____

Name (Mr. or Ms.) _____

Address_____

City_____ State_____ Zip_____

Mail to...New Day Christian Education, Inc. PO Box 30821, Greenville, NC 27833

New Day
Christian Education, Inc.

Prayer Request (s):

Mail to...New Day Christian Education, Inc. PO Box 30821, Greenville, NC 27833

Workshop/Seminar Evaluation

Date _____ Full Name (optional) _____

Name of the workshop/seminar that you attended

_____

Who were the speakers? (If other than Merlin and Shawner English) _____

Evaluation of Content and Format

Relevance to my everyday life	Low	Med	High
Relevance to my Christian walk	Low	Med	High
Appropriateness of training methods & materials	Low	Med	High

Comments & Suggestions

_____

_____

_____

Evaluation of Delivery

Knowledge of subject	Low	Med	High
Teaching skills	Low	Med	High
Facilities	Poor	Med	Great

Comments & Suggestions

_____

_____

_____

Suggested Changes (What would you change to make this workshop/seminar more effective?)

_____
_____
_____
_____
_____
_____
_____
_____
_____
_____
_____
_____
_____
_____
_____
_____
_____
_____
_____
_____
_____
_____